R

BUSINESS, ADMINISTRATION & FINANCE

ANGELA YOUNGMAN

Real Life Guide to Business, Administration & Finance

This first edition published in 2009 by Trotman Publishing, an imprint of Crimson Publishing, Westminster House, Kew Road, Richmond, Surrey TW9 2ND

© Trotman Publishing 2009

Author: Angela Youngman

British Library Cataloguing in Publication Data
A catalogue record for this book is available from the British Library

ISBN: 978-1-84455-222-1

Typeset by RefineCatch Ltd, Bungay, Suffolk

Printed and bound in Italy by LEGO SpA

CONTENTS

FOREWORD

This *Real Life Guide to Business, Administration & Finance* offers practical information on every aspect of training for and finding a job in the field. Whether you are just starting out or looking for your next career move, this book shows the different entry routes into the industry, gives you an outline of the jobs available, and explains the skills and attributes you need to be successful.

City & Guilds vocational qualifications support learners from pre-entry to professional level and we award over a million certificates every year. Our qualifications meet the latest industry requirements and are recognised by employers worldwide as proof that candidates have the knowledge and skills to get the job done.

We are delighted to be a part of the Trotman *Real Life Guides* series to help raise your awareness of these vocational qualifications – we are confident that they can help you to achieve excellence and quality in whichever field you choose. For more information about the courses City & Guilds offers check out www.cityandguilds.com – get yourself qualified and see what you could do.

City & Guilds

ABOUT THE AUTHOR

Angela Youngman is a qualified teacher working as a freelance journalist and author. She specialises in leisure, education, careers and gardening. Angela has written several books, including a series of 'How to' gardening books. As a journalist she has undertaken editorial work on a wide range of topics for numerous publications, as well as writing and compiling websites. She is married, has two children and lives in Norfolk.

ACKNOWLEDGEMENTS

The author wishes to thank PGL, Kellogg's, The National Trust, The Prince's Trust and other organisations for their help with case studies and background information.

INTRODUCTION

Do you want a career that is challenging and offers untold opportunities to move from one business area to another with ease? Then look no further. That is precisely what careers in business, administration and finance offer. Skills learned in this sector are infinitely flexible and ensure that you never have to worry about your skill set being too specific. These skills offer a good foundation for a very wide range of careers and professions.

Business, administration and finance offers the widest possible range of careers, ranging from receptionists to managerial staff, payroll clerks to financial advisors. For people prepared to work hard and develop skills, a career in this sector can be a very interesting option. There is a constant demand for staff at all levels.

The majority of businesses in the UK are small or medium sized enterprises. The days of domination of industry by a few large employers have gone. This sector is constantly changing, not only in what it does but also in the companies involved. This means that there are always new opportunities appearing and that very few people will stay with one employer for all their working lives. Consequently, throughout your career you will need to update your skills to take advantage of new opportunities. If you do not do this you can get left behind. According to the Council for Administration, 97% of all employers state that business administration is critical to the effective functioning of their business, while 40% of employers state that they find it a challenge to recruit suitably qualified and trained administration staff.

It is one of the most flexible areas in which to work. Skills are easily transferable and it is possible to move from local government to private enterprise, develop your own company or be self-employed, to work for charities and other non-profit making enterprises or to work for public organisations. A wide range of skills can be acquired and your career can take many new paths at any stage in your working life. There is a wide range of jobs available – administrators, office workers and business people are always needed. Even in the public sector, there is continuous internal reorganisation with some areas expanding and others declining. To take maximum advantage of this you will need flexibility and mobility.

Careers in business, finance and administration can offer opportunities for travel or overseas work as well as work within the UK.

Jobs covered in the business, finance and administration sector fall into 6 groups:

1. public service
2. private enterprise
3. not for profit organisations
4. service industries
5. financial services
6. self-employment.

There is also a huge core range of jobs that are common to all sectors, such as administrators, payroll clerks, secretaries and personal assistants.

So is a career in business, finance and administration for you? If you have the right skills, then the answer could well be yes.

You need to be calm, able to work in a team as well as on your own. Being able to use your initiative, an ability to accept responsibility and to get on with all kinds of people are other useful attributes. You can find out more about the skills required to work in business, finance and administration in Chapter 6, Tools of the Trade.

You have to be able to deal with people as well as systems; be able to accept routine work and enjoy working in an office environment. Numeracy, good communication and IT skills are important.

To find out more about potential career opportunities browse through the pages of this book. It will highlight the types of careers that can be found, including details of training and future prospects. There are case studies of people working in the sector, talking about their jobs and how they have developed interesting careers. There is also a fun quiz to see how much you really know about business, administration and finance!

Also included are sections on how to find out whether you have the right personal qualities to make a successful career in business, finance and administration, as well as lots of contact addresses and websites of professional organisations and training providers for you to find out more.

CHAPTER 1
SUCCESS STORY

HEATHER WILLIAMS

Practitioner at Kellogg's

Heather Williams has been working at Kellogg's for over 20 years in many different teams and roles. She started as a temporary office worker and has since developed her career into many different activities.

'I initially joined as a temp in the finance department for two weeks. The role I was covering was vacant and within a few weeks I became a permanent member of the treasury department. After that I moved across to our internal catering department as Stock Controller and Buyer in the canteen, buying and maintaining stock levels and negotiating with suppliers. I then moved to our Wrexham plant within production scheduling, before working in demand planning where I had to ensure that all elements of demand were captured and built into forecasts for manufacturing to see and produce against. [Basically this means she is involved in forecasting future sales so that the production line produces the required amounts of individual products, to avoid shortages or stockpiling.]

'I then transferred into the business execution planning team to co-ordinate forecast to fulfilment with a full "end to end" process of supply, from manufacturing to our customers. We work closely with our demand planning teams to understand what's driving the forecasts, what impact TV and media campaigns are likely to have and what's happening in innovation – such as new products due to be launched within the next 12 months. As there are so many different areas and challenges, no two days are the same. However, I do try to plan effectively to ensure that there aren't too many surprises. This role gave me the opportunity to interact with a lot of different teams across the organisation.

'I presented to the sales team every week to keep them informed of supply risks, product concerns and service levels. Communication is the key here and we're all constantly learning. We work closely with supply chain and sales and marketing to deliver their needs and maintain a high service level to our customers.

'Following this role, I undertook a 15-month secondment as Planning and Project Lead at our portable foods site in Wrexham where we make a range of bars for the snacks market, before undertaking the role I'm in now.

'In February 2009, I transferred to the Manchester plant to the role of Packing Area Co-ordinator and have since been seconded into a practitioner role to train and support our operators during the project initiative a number of our plants are currently working through.

'There is a real "can-do" attitude at Kellogg's and the benefits are great. You can move around departments and locations and the opportunities are endless. I've enjoyed tremendous support from my managers over the years and they've been great at helping me to expand my knowledge of the business and identify which directions I should take throughout my career. I'm hoping to enjoy many more years here.'

CHAPTER 2
WHAT'S THE STORY?

Business, administration and finance is by far the largest
employment area within the UK economy covering as it does
so many different sectors from transport to manufacturing,
government to financial services. It covers everything from one
person working from home to the big multinational corporations
with hundreds of offices worldwide. Small businesses and start up
businesses make a major contribution to the economy, increasing
the number of jobs, productivity and prosperity.

The UK is predominantly a nation of small businesses. If you add
the number of self-employed and small businesses with under
5 employees, there are probably around 5 million businesses. But
there are less than 12,000 businesses which employ more than
250 people and a further 26,000 which employ between 100 and
250 people.

Around 5 million people are now employed in administration,
business and financial office work. This figure is expected to rise
as it is a sector destined to substantially expand in future years.
There is always demand for skilled staff with work opportunities
available on a permanent or temporary basis. Around 40% of
employers are reported to have difficulty finding skilled business
and administrative staff.

Until 2009, the last decade has seen growth in the numbers of
businesses in every sector and the number of people employed.

TABLE 1

OFFICE FOR NATIONAL STATISTICS 2008 FIGURES ON UK BUSINESS (BY SECTOR)

Sector	Number of workers
Agriculture	154,015
Production	151,720
Construction	232,640
Motor trades	71,320
Wholesale	109,355
Retail	199,290
Hotels and catering	133,300
Transport	65,840
Post and telecommunications	16,320
Finance	31,365
Property and business services	658,795
Education	27,800
Health	77,165
Public administration and other services	170,090

PUBLIC SERVICE

Public service involves a wide range of organisations including the local and national government, Armed Forces, National Health Service, housing associations, police, fire and ambulance services. It is a massive sector covering everything from security to refuse collection, administering elections and payrolls to working with police officers. Funds to operate these services and pay staff salaries is raised through taxation. Government initiatives often require new people to put the initiatives into practice, and to administer and organise

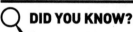

DID YOU KNOW?

There are over 2,077,190 people working in local government alone.

LOCAL GOVERNMENT

Local government in England and Wales is funded by grants from central government (approximately 48%), business rates (paid by local companies, which accounts for approximately 25% of income), and council tax (which is paid by people living within the area of the local council and also accounts for about 25% of the overall total). The remainder of the money comes from sources such as council owned car parks, parking permits and the hire of sports facilities.

schemes. There is a long-term need for good administrators capable of organising and working in large public organisations.

Local government is a huge public service provider covering everything from education to environmental health, housing to social services as well as heritage, libraries, markets and refuse collection. It spends over £70bn a year providing services. In total there are 27 county councils, 33 London boroughs, 36 metropolitan councils, 201 district councils, 56 English unitary councils, 32 Scottish unitary councils, 22 Welsh unitary councils and 26 Northern Irish district councils.

Local government is made up of elected councillors, who decide policy, and council staff who deliver the services based on those policies. The council staff are also required to provide information which councillors can use to make decisions. There are around 600 occupations and thousands of different job titles in local government.

Civil service and central government are the same thing – civil servants work for the government in power dealing with national policies on education, defence, finance and so on.

There used to be a simple split between public and private enterprise. But most public organisations have contracted out services to private businesses. For example, many councils have contracted out payroll, refuse collection and the running of care homes. NHS hospitals have a wide range of contracted-out services and over the years this sub-sector will increase.

PRIVATE ENTERPRISE

This covers all types of manufacturing and enterprise activities owned by private individuals or organisations. The government is keen to encourage private enterprise because it sees this as the means by which the UK economy will grow in the foreseeable future. Although heavy industry such as shipbuilding and mining has declined, there has been a steady growth in companies producing computer software, engineering, packaging and distribution, internet businesses, clothing, food and beverages.

New businesses are constantly being set up as people identify an unfilled niche in the market. Many of these are small companies which will grow over time. A large number of businesses have a short shelf life as the opportunity they exploited comes and goes. For example, when video became popular, there was a rush of businesses selling or renting videos; when DVDs replaced videos, the reason for existence of these businesses disappeared. Getting involved in small, growing companies can provide useful career opportunities since you can develop your career alongside the company. In recent years, many of these companies have been operating via the internet with people setting up businesses selling products such as t-shirts solely via internet sites. Such internet ventures are expected to increase still further as more and more people prefer to work from home, or via small independent businesses.

The popularity of television programmes such as *Dragons' Den* and *The Apprentice* indicates the popularity of business careers. Such programmes show just how enterprising people can be, coming up with innovative solutions and business ideas such as selling shoes by party plan, creating light up drinking glasses, a device to stop you putting the wrong type of fuel in your car and special plug in safety lights. Banks and investors are willing to back projects which have a clear cut business plan and most new start up businesses survive.

The world of business is constantly changing. It can be affected by outside factors such as the economic climate, political events, changes in production, the oil crisis, environmental affairs as well as consumer demand. The names of companies change too – sometimes reflecting changes in ownership or simply corporate policy such as the change from Norwich Union Insurance to Aviva.

NOT FOR PROFIT ORGANISATIONS

This is a constantly expanding sector covering everything from traditional charities such as Save the Children, RSPCA, RSPB, Cancer Research and Oxfam to heritage organisations like the National Trust; one off appeals in response to a major disaster or famine; and fundraising activities by schools and special not for profit organisations set up to promote interest in topics such as green consumerism, organic gardening and the environment. Churches and other religious organisations require administrators to organise their day to day activities. Organisations like The Prince's Trust are charities. Some are high profile and well known, while others are quietly working in the background and seeking to make an impact. It is a way in which you can make an active contribution to society and earn a living at the same time.

While all charities use a large number of volunteers at local level, this army of volunteers needs professional management and administration at local, regional and national level.

SERVICE INDUSTRIES

This is another growth area. It deals with a vast range of businesses which provide some kind of service to other businesses or to the general public or to the public sector. A service industry is one where no goods are produced. It covers a very broad set of industries including nurseries, cleaning, business services such as waste disposal, catering, computing, software, property management and transactions, tourism, storage, transport and travel, recreation and entertainment, leisure, distribution, retailing, personal services such as hairdressing, domestic cleaning and funerals. There is a large proportion of highly skilled and highly technological jobs, with business opportunities expanding and new niche markets appearing all the time. Service industries generate approximately two thirds of all jobs in developed countries and their importance is growing.

FINANCIAL SERVICES

Financial services are among the UK's most successful business sectors and have a world wide reputation. London is the financial capital of the world.

As a sector, it includes retail and wholesale banking, credit finance, investment, insurance, accountancy, share dealing on the Stock Exchange, foreign exchange, mortgage and pensions. Its products are used by most people in the country – everyone needs insurance if they drive a car, finance is needed to buy a house and salaries have to be paid into banks. As a sector it is constantly innovating, devising solutions to changing situations such as ethical insurance and investment, Islamic finance and globalisation.

LONDON FINANCE

- London is the world's leading financial centre where every leading financial institution on the planet is represented. A third of the world's largest companies have their headquarters there. It is also home to more than 40 billionaires.
- It is the world's largest foreign exchange market with a daily turnover of US$1.47 billion representing some 34% of the global market. More euros are traded in the London market than in all the euro-areas combined.
- The London Stock Exchange is the most international of all the world's stock exchanges with around 3,000 companies from all over the world admitted to its markets. It has grown from small beginnings within the coffee houses of seventeenth century London and in 2007 it merged with the Borsa Italiana, creating Europe's leading diversified exchange business: the London Stock Exchange Group.

The insurance sector is a major player offering a wide range of services from car and house insurance to pensions, life cover and savings. It is the largest in Europe and is now the second largest insurance business in the world. There are 1,017 companies authorised to carry out insurance business in the UK employing 309,000 people – about a third of all financial services jobs and twice as many as are employed in motor vehicle manufacturing and the electricity, gas and water supply sectors. It is a sector that is constantly changing, as the way people buy insurance has changed dramatically over the past 10 years.

DID YOU KNOW?

Within London alone there are around 4,000 banks of which 160 have a staff roll of more than 250 employees. Other big financial centres within the UK include Leeds, Edinburgh, Birmingham, Manchester and Glasgow. Within Scotland, financial services account for 1 in 10 jobs.

In general fewer people are buying insurance through brokers; instead they are going to banks and building societies, while most life and pensions business is now sold by independent financial advisors.

Banking employs around half a million people, while the wider financial services industry employs over 1.1 million. When you add in all the related activities such as accountancy and business services around 3 million people rely on the financial sector for their jobs.

Turning to other aspects of the financial services industry, there are now 53 building societies within the UK possessing total assets of over £385bn, while the investment banking sector is steadily growing. This sector deals with corporate banking and investment management as well as securities trading, business mergers, takeovers and acquisitions. Most investment bank career opportunities start at A level or with business studies diplomas. Accountancy is a major market sector. Every company and organisation, public, private and not for profit require the services of accountants. Steve Priddy, a director of the Association of Chartered Certified Accountants, says:

> 'There has never been a more crucial time for accountants to continue to show their true value. Over the past 18 months, as a systemic banking collapse has evolved into significant worldwide recession in many countries, we believe that the role of the accountant will emerge as a champion of sustainable value in business. Accountants are advocates of sound business practice, champions of sustainable business development and identifiers of value drivers which lead to high performing organisations.'

Productivity within the financial sector is increasing at a rate of three times to that of the UK economy as a whole. It is set to continue growing.

SELF-EMPLOYMENT

Many people want to be self-employed or set up their own business. Banks and government departments estimate that there are up to 3 million self-employed people working from home, and up to 5 million small businesses with no employees in the UK.

There are more being set up every day. It can take as little as 6 months for a business to be set up from scratch. Banks are keen to provide finance for small businesses – over 80% of applications from first time businesses are approved. Such businesses can be extremely successful. Over 80% of new businesses survive their first year of trading.

The development of electronic technology such as the internet and video conferencing means that many new businesses and self-employed people no longer

DID YOU KNOW?

The Coca-Cola company was founded in 1892 when inventor John Pemberton came up with a unique recipe. It gained its name because the drink contained cocaine and caffeine (from cola nuts). Needless to say, the drink no longer contains cocaine! The popularity of the drink took off after the Second World War and it is now a household name in almost every country in the world.

have to have an office in the nearest town or city. This has led to a huge upsurge in working from home, or from small offices in villages. Many country villages and towns have been revived due to the internet revolution. This also has huge cost advantages for the sector as there is no longer a need to rent expensive offices in town. For those looking forward in their career there are other opportunities in that part time and flexible working can mean businesses can continue or be set up, to work around the needs of family life.

THE FUTURE

Versatility is extremely important in business. To survive, businesses need to be quick to react to developments of all kinds. Production methods are constantly changing and new inventions are always coming on stream. Take video tapes for example: this was a massive industry for about 30 years, but has now almost completely been replaced by DVDs. This has affected not just recording organisations and film companies, but packaging, advertising, design, and retail as well. New solutions are constantly being sought to changing economic or production conditions.

The 2009 HSBC Future of Business report indicated that British industry is set for a major transformation, with the country becoming a leading proponent of video games, superfoods and robotics. According to the report, factories and power stations will be supplanted by centres for gaming, windfarms and robotics as the economic landscape is redrawn around the next generation of industries. It is forecasting a new regional geography with the birth of five new super cities and a map of tomorrow populated by nanotech, cybernetics and a growing emphasis on bio and tech sciences. According to the report's authors, the changes will create an emphasis on interpersonal skills in business, technological advances, the demands of many for new and flexible ways of working, more business trade taking place across international borders and a rise in entrepreneurship.

According to the research there will be a new look UK with business hubs focusing on:

- ▶ robotics – Edinburgh, Birmingham, Essex, London, Manchester, Plymouth
- ▶ biotech – York and Dundee
- ▶ nanotech – Oxford, Cambridge, Newcastle, Durham, Bristol, London

- ▶ stem cell research – Edinburgh, London, Cambridge, Liverpool, Manchester
- ▶ nutraceuticals – Dundee, Southampton
- ▶ renewable energies – London, Wales, Cornwall, Glasgow
- ▶ cybernetics – Reading
- ▶ gaming – Dundee, Edinburgh, Glasgow.

For people working in the sector, one of the biggest advantages to a career in business, administration and finance is the simple fact that it covers so many activities. Operating computers, organising an office, keeping basic accounts, writing reports and letters, dealing with customers are the same whatever business you are in. This means you can work in all kinds of different types of business. Skills learned in one area of business such as in an insurance office can be used to obtain work in places like tourist organisations, travel companies, manufacturing companies, accountants and newspapers, to name but a few. It is a very flexible career option.

DID YOU KNOW?

In 1943 Thomas Watson, chairman of IBM, predicted that there would be a world market for just five computers. He could not have been more wrong. There are now over 1 billion computers in use worldwide and numbers are constantly increasing.

Business and administration skills are vital to the success of any organisation. Without these skills, businesses could not exist. There is great demand for well trained people, and it is predicted that the number of opportunities will continue to increase substantially for the foreseeable future. Choosing a career in this sector does not mean confining yourself to a low level office job – you can progress as far as you like and work in sectors that appeal to you whether it is being a secretary in a record company, an administrator in the civil service or a financial controller in a large manufacturing business.

CHAPTER 3
QUIZ

If you've read through the last few pages, you should have quite a good idea as to whether you're interested in a career in business, administration and finance. If you think you are, why not test your knowledge and suitability a little further by completing the following short quiz. For each question, just choose which option you think is correct or the closest to what you think your response would be, and compare it with the answers at the end of the chapter. Don't worry if you get any questions wrong, it's only meant to be a bit of fun.

1 When was the system we know as (www.) set up?
A. 1981
B. 1991
C. 2001

2 What is meant by conveyancing?
A. Transporting food across the country
B. A method of transport
C. Transferring ownership of property such as houses from one person to another

3 Which business revolutionised fast food?
A. McDonald's
B. Burger King
C. Kentucky Fried Chicken

4 What is a patent?

A. A computer

B. A type of food

C. Exclusive rights to a product granted to an inventor

5 What is the oldest UK company?

A. C Hoare & Co

B. The Shore Porter's Society

C. James Lock & Co

6 Apple and IBM are

A. Fruit

B. Computer manufacturers

C. Cars

7 How many cheques are cleared each day by the main high street banks?

A. 7 million

B. 8 million

C. 9 million

8 VAT is an abbreviation for

A. Vans and taxis

B. Value added tax

C. Vague and troubled

9 A limited company is a business that:

A. Is limited in what it can do

B. Is limited in what it can sell

C. Is a legal entity

10 Which of following three well known businessmen has not appeared in an advert for his company?

A. Richard Branson

B. Bernard Matthews

C. Rupert Murdoch

11 What is a CEO?
A. A children's entertainment officer
B. A chief executive officer
C. A clerical expenses officer

12 How many cheques are processed every ten minutes by British banks?
A. 10,000
B. 20,000
C. 25,000

13 What is Lloyd's of London?
A. A bank
B. A group of insurance syndicates
C. A pharmacy

ANSWERS

1. B. The World Wide Web (www.) was launched in 1991, only a year after it had first been described by Tim Berners-Lee. It is a system which combines pictures, words and sounds in an easily understood form accessible to anyone. The phrase 'surfing the net' also appeared for the first time in 1991.

2. C. Conveyancing is undertaken by solicitors. It is part of the legal system and deals with the preparation of documents relating to the buying and selling of property such as houses and firms.

3. A. In 1961, Ray Kroc brought a hamburger stand owned by the McDonald brothers in California for $2.7m which turned out to be one of the biggest bargains of the twentieth century. He quickly expanded this business. Within two years, the famous golden arches of McDonald's could be found all over America. Now it is a worldwide business.

4. C. A patent is exclusive rights granted to an inventor of a product. It enables the inventor to make money by developing the invention without the risk of a rival stealing the idea.

5. B. The Shore Porter's Society was established in 1498. An Aberdeen co-operative, it claims to be the oldest established transport contractor in the UK, and possibly in the world. C Hoare & Co is a private bank founded in 1672, while James Lock & Co is a hat company founded in 1676.

6. B. All computer systems in the world either work on an Apple or IBM format. Although the two rivals now make it easier for computers to use either format, both keep the process complex enough so that in practice the two systems are not compatible.

7. C. Up to 9 million cheques are cleared each day. The cheques are cleared by checking to ensure there is enough money in the account of the person who has written the cheque before transferring the money to the account of the person being paid. This is why banks like Barclays, National Westminster, Lloyds, HSBC and Co-op are also known as clearing banks.

8. B. Value Added Tax is a sales tax imposed on most products and services sold in the UK.

9. C. All limited companies have boards of directors and have to file annual accounts with Companies House.

10. C. Media mogul Rupert Murdoch is the odd one out as both of the others have appeared in adverts for their companies. Richard Branson is boss of the Virgin Group while Bernard Matthews is best known for his turkey farms and food production companies.

11. B. A CEO is a chief executive officer and is responsible for running a company.

12. C. Banking systems process 25,000 cheques every 10 minutes. They also do 102,000 automatic credits and 123,000 plastic card payments in the same period; pay out nearly £3m of cash via ATMs and respond to 8,500 customer account queries by phone plus 40,000 queries online.

13. B. Lloyd's of London is a market where members join together as syndicates to insure risks. There are 80 syndicates in all which form the world's largest insurance market. Lloyd's started out dealing only with marine insurance but now the market covers some of the world's largest and most complex risks including oil rigs, bridges, airlines and even celebrity body parts. It can accept risks from over 200 countries.

CHAPTER 4
WHAT ARE THE JOBS?

Employment opportunities within the business, finance and administration sector are wide ranging and numerous. No matter what the job, every one involves using computers, office equipment and spending a large time of the day in an office. It offers tremendous opportunities to follow your own interests and inclinations. Some people prefer working for large companies or organisations; others prefer small businesses; some prefer to work for public organisations while others prefer private enterprise or charities.

There are opportunities in almost every aspect of business you can think of – insurance, manufacturing, tourism, leisure, banking, farms, councils, civil service, media, transport, retailing and commerce, to name but a few. Job opportunities are constantly increasing and are forecast to continue growing for the foreseeable future.

Modern technology means that people in offices around the UK can talk to each other online, using emails, video conferencing and a host of other modern technologies. This does mean that many office jobs will change over the next few years. Modern technology plus environmental pressure on all sectors, means that business travel will reduce over the years. Although not yet common, there is a view that efficient businesses will rapidly reduce the amount of face to face meetings, that often waste a huge amount of time and travel, and replace these with electronic means. These factors combined mean that those working in an office will spend more and more time at their desks.

So what types of job exist?

JOBS COMMON TO ALL SECTORS

There is a core range of jobs which are common to all business sectors no matter what type of industry or organisation is involved. The titles may be different but the types of tasks are fairly similar. For example, someone working for another person or persons and dealing with all their administration can be described in various ways – secretary, personal secretary, assistant, executive assistant, administrative assistant, personal assistant, clerical assistant, administrator, girl/gal/man Friday, clerk. Sometimes two people in the same office may have the same title, but have slightly different functions. For example there may be two secretaries but one is slightly more experienced than the other and is expected to do more confidential work as well as supervising the second secretary. Their salaries could well be virtually identical.

◯ DID YOU KNOW?

Internet use has grown in popularity faster than any other form of communication. In just over 10 years, it has become a global phenomenon. In 1994, around 20 million people used the internet – now there are well over one and half billion users and it is still growing.

Opportunities for administrators, secretaries, telephonists, payroll clerks and receptionists can be found in all business sectors. Every company and organisation needs people to work on reception desks dealing with visitors and general phone calls. Payroll staff are needed to manage pay and benefits systems everywhere staff are employed. There are vast numbers of people working in these roles. To take just one example – medical secretaries. There are around 30,000 medical secretaries in the UK working in the public service within NHS hospitals, community health, GP surgeries and health centres. In addition, there are numerous other employment opportunities within private enterprise and not for profit organisations such as within private medical institutions, medical research, the pharmaceutical industry, medical charities and complementary medicine.

In general, starting salaries are around £11,000. Depending on skills, qualifications and the sector in which you are working this can rise ultimately to around £25,000+.

Working for an agency on a temporary basis (as a 'temp') can result in higher salary rates but they do require some prior skill and business knowledge. However, it is important to remember that for temporary staff, there is no job security and no benefits such as pensions or holiday pay. A temporary job lasts only as long as the booking is required which can be as short as a week. You then have to wait for another temporary job to arise, usually within a different company. There are lots of advantages to working as a temp. Temporary work is a good way of experiencing a variety of business sectors. Often it can be a means of trying out a potential job before accepting it on a permanent basis; or it can lead to offers of work elsewhere within a company.

PUBLIC SERVICE

Public service refers to organisations whose role is involved in serving the public. It is a very large sector and includes national and local government, police authorities, fire authorities, Customs & Excise and the National Health Service – both within hospitals and doctors surgeries. There is a vast range of jobs available including secretaries, administrative assistants and office managers, and good staff are always needed. It offers stable employment with good prospects for promotion.

Many jobs within local and national government are advertised on the JobCentre Plus website. Experience and skills count just as much as academic qualifications. It is possible to enter as an administrative trainee or assistant and develop a career in many different ways as there are numerous specialist roles available. This is true of any public service organisation.

Typical specialist administrative and business roles range from working as a registrar of births, deaths, marriages and civil partnerships to being a local government markets officer, a revenue officer, a regeneration manager or an elections officer. Such roles have specific responsibilities, for example an elections officer is responsible for updating the electoral database as well as booking buildings to use as polling stations and overseeing the electoral process. A markets officer on the other hand is responsible for the smooth running of markets and street trading within a specific area and has to collect rents, deal with issues and problems that arise, writing reports and making sure that traders work within the terms of their contracts.

Daily tasks vary considerably according to the job involved. A business administration trainee in local government for example may be involved with a wide range of tasks such as inputting financial data, running queries in the financial system, maintenance and updating of hard copy and electronic financial filing systems, providing administrative support to different teams, answering telephone calls, taking messages, word processing, formatting letters and reports, carrying out general duties such as photocopying, printing, faxing, collating and distributing the post.

Yet in another county someone with exactly the same job title may be responsible for carrying out administrative tasks, compiling reports about performance statistics, and dealing with complaints. This can involve considerable personal contact with the public, especially when it comes to dealing with complaints, as well as the pressure of meeting deadlines for reports.

To take another example of work in local government, a revenues assistant for a council could be involved in making payment arrangements, dealing with reminders, final notices, summonses and liability orders, taking recovery action on accounts, contacting bailiffs, issuing attachment of earnings/benefit orders and monitoring bailiff arrangements. This could also be dealing with purchase orders and approving invoices, minuting meetings, providing court support, and answering queries on council tax and business rates.

The police authorities use a lot of civilian support staff to undertake jobs like receptionists, document submissions officers, team leaders, researchers. Previous work experience is required, and this can be obtained in any administrative or financial capacity.

Starting salaries for an administrative assistant are generally in the region of £11,000 and with experience this can rise to around £20,000. Salaries for specialist functions are much higher. For example, a markets officer can earn up to £31,000 a year while registrars have a salary range between £16,000 and £40,000 a year. European Union assistants working in Brussels start on £27,000, while a local government revenues officer can earn up to £33,000 or more.

PRIVATE ENTERPRISE

From manufacturing to distribution, transport to building there is a vast range of companies employing staff to administer and organise their operations. Apart from general administrative positions, there are many specialist roles which can provide an interesting and challenging career. Quality managers for example

---

FROM LITTLE ACORNS...

The Tesco Group grew out of a market stall owned by Jack Cohen and is now the UK's largest retailer, and a multi national business. Apart from its supermarkets, Tesco's now has its own bank and insurance facilities and operates in many different countries. Its annual turnover exceeds the gross national income of many small countries.

---

are essential to all manufacturing businesses since they are responsible for ensuring that all products meet required quality standards. It is up to the quality manager to put systems in place to ensure consistency, then to monitor and advise on how the systems are performing. Project managers are needed to supervise and lead special projects, developing plans, overseeing finances and monitoring progress. A distribution manager is responsible for ensuring the distribution of products takes place smoothly and efficiently to set deadlines. This can involve administering transport fleets, drivers and fuel requirements, as well as the actual movement of products being manufactured by a company.

Another example is that of company secretary. With experience and training, it is possible to move into the role of company secretary. Despite the name this does not refer to a typical secretarial role writing letters and working for one or more executives. Company secretaries have a pivotal role in a business, being involved in all general management decisions as well as having to have a knowledge of the law and finance. It is the responsibility of the company secretary to ensure that a company always acts within the boundaries of the law.

Salaries for specialist roles are much higher than for general ones, often starting at around £22,000 or more and rising to £60,000 or more. This reflects the need to obtain specialist qualifications before taking up these roles.

Another key sector is that of entrepreneur. Anyone of any age can become an entrepreneur. You need a good idea, business acumen, to be self-motivated, confident and willing to work very hard. It can be extremely challenging and rewarding for the right people. Entrepreneurs work for themselves in their own business. There are thousands of different types of business and tasks vary according to the nature of the business. The government regards enterprise of this kind as the key to future economic growth and gives it considerable support as do organisations like The Prince's Trust and Young Enterprise. Businesses can be started from

ENTREPRENEUR

Businesses use millions of Post-it notes. There are even Stickies which can be used as part of computer programs. The whole idea came from an invention by Dr Spencer Silver who worked for the 3M company. He created an adhesive backing which sticks but leaves no residue when the object is removed. He could see no use for it so he left it alone for several years. Then in 1974, his colleague Arthur Fry used the adhesive on a bookmark. The rest is history – people started asking questions and soon 3M had launched the first Post-it notes.

scratch, or you can buy a franchise or existing business. Some people start a business straight from school, others seek to gain some experience first.

Major businesses can come from very small beginnings as the example of Fraser Doherty shows. He set up a company called Superjam based on his grandmother's recipes. Unusually, the jam does not contain any sugar and relies on the fruit for its sweetness. 'I began making it when I was 14. I sold my first jars to neighbours; then sold them at local fêtes and farmers' markets. I was really excited by it. It soon got to the point where I was making about a thousand jars a week from my parents' tiny kitchen. They couldn't get in there to cook so I started to use a factory in England. It's been a real adventure to go so far from such tiny beginnings.' By the time he was 19, his company was producing 500,000 jars of jam annually and was supplying Superjam to over a thousand supermarkets around Britain including Waitrose. Doherty is now planning to enter the American market.

'Superjam was funded almost entirely organically. I reinvested profits back into the company as it grew. I also got a small loan from The Prince's Trust. I got help from Scottish Enterprise, who set up an initial meeting with a supermarket buyer at a "meet the buyer" event that they run where I got 10 minutes to pitch Superjam to the senior buyer from Waitrose. I also got help from entrepreneurs who had already built successful companies and were willing to mentor me, giving up maybe an hour of their time every couple of months to give me advice and so on.

'Superjam is growing at an amazing pace, at least doubling year on year. We now supply Tesco, Asda, Morrisons, Waitrose and Sainsburys.'

Superjam for example has developed its own charity 'The SuperJam Tea Parties' as Fraser Doherty explains. 'We run tea parties for lonely elderly people. We have live music, free food and drinks and the opportunity for the guests to have fun and make new friends. The events typically attract up to 300 people. We've run over 100 events, mostly in Scotland, and the charity is now starting to grow nationally, hopefully benefiting thousands, or even tens of thousands, of lonely and isolated elderly people.'

CHOCOLATE HEAVEN

Production of Cadbury chocolate began at Bournville in 1879. It has since become a global business with factories all over the world. The Cadbury production line runs 24 hours a day, 7 days a week, 364 days per year. The Cadbury Crème Egg production line makes 600,000 eggs every 12 hour shift – roughly the weight of 3 elephants! If all the Cadbury Crème Eggs made each year were laid end to end, they would circle the planet, while enough Cadbury Dairy Milk is sold each year to cover every Premiership and Championship football pitch – five times over.

NOT FOR PROFIT

Working for not for profit organisations can give a big sense of achievement and satisfaction to your work. You are helping to give something back to society, helping to solve a problem or increase awareness of a specific issue. For someone committed to a particular charity or belief careers in this sector can be very rewarding. There are numerous opportunities available to develop a career. Most entry level opportunities are for secretarial, clerical, or administrative assistant positions. With experience and training, it is possible to move into senior positions such as administrators or financial controllers. Specialist roles include working as appeals administrators, school bursars and business managers. This is a major growth area with new positions and new charities constantly arising.

This can prove to be a very challenging career for people able to control budgets and deal with administration, who possess good communication skills and have an inventive, flexible mind open to opportunities. Often, it involves working on your own or in a very small team seeking creative ways of raising money for a specific cause. Successful professional fund raisers are much in demand.

Within both state and independent schools, business managers are becoming an increasingly familiar sight charged with the responsibility of raising funds by renting out facilities such as sports halls, gyms, halls and classrooms as well as seeking sponsorship, doing business deals and organising all kinds of events from fêtes to abseils.

Salaries tend to be slightly lower when working for not for profit organisations. Entry level salaries are around £10,000 and can rise to around £30,000 depending on qualifications and the type of job. The size of the charity or organisation can also affect the salary level – a small charity will not be able to afford to pay as much as a large, well known charity simply because its income level will be lower.

SERVICE INDUSTRIES

Service industries are widespread and cover a vast range of opportunities. It covers all kinds of companies which offer a service to businesses or the consumer such as recruitment, law, retail, tourism, marketing, public relations, utilities, graphic design, advertising, TV and media. The arrival of the internet has widened the scope still further with the creation of jobs to run internet sites, software organisations and internet service providers.

Job opportunities throughout all forms of the service industry are considerable. This is a sector which is constantly increasing with new companies being founded or existing businesses expanding. Apart from general administrative, managerial and secretarial jobs there are numerous specialist opportunities such as recruitment advisors and employment consultants who help companies fill job vacancies by matching the vacancy with job hunters. Such work requires a knowledge of the industry as well as good communication skills. This is a big area – over 100,000 people work in recruitment. Sometimes people use it as a stepping stone in their own career development or set up their own agencies.

Management consultants are much in demand by businesses trying to find ways of improving productivity and efficiency, or to suggest ways of dealing with problems that have arisen. Competition for such jobs is intense and it is very much confined to graduates with specialist qualifications. However, such companies also need large numbers of administrators and secretaries in order to deal with day to day concerns.

Other work opportunities include business advisors, sales and marketing managers, systems analysts, careers advisors, paralegals, legal executives and licensed conveyancers.

Salaries vary from job to job. Recruitment advisors usually start at around £17,000 rising to £35,000+ with experience. Often this includes commission or performance related bonuses.

Management consultants start at £25,000 and rise to over £50,000. Depending on the company or service involved, there may be additional benefits such as staff discounts, low cost insurance, cheap mortgages, free banking or cheap travel.

FINANCIAL SERVICES

Opportunities within the financial services sector are wide ranging. No two jobs are the same. Talented people are much in demand and there are good promotion prospects. In insurance, career opportunities range from claims investigation and settlement; processing administrators responsible for transferring information into electronic systems and keeping records up to date; broking administrators identifying and explaining standard insurance products; to customers then organising the proposal forms. Investment advisors play an important role in handling records and measuring investment performance while account reconciliation administrators monitor transactions being processed and reconcile these with client accounts, liaising where necessary to resolve queries and discrepancies.

DID YOU KNOW?

The dollar is the world's most common currency, followed by the euro, pound, dinar, peso and rupee.

Banking is a much wider than just the activities of cashiers and customer service advisors seen within every high street bank or building society. There are also opportunities to work as foreign currency advisors identifying methods of transferring funds overseas or in corporate finance. Careers can be developed into supervisory or specialist roles.

Accountancy offers opportunities to work in auditing, book keeping, payroll and financial management, as well as specialisms such as insolvency management and tax consultancy. There are also opportunities in credit finance and leasing and as financial advisors providing guidance on a range of products such as mortgages, pensions and investments.

Then there are opportunities to develop careers working in foreign exchange or getting involved in share dealing, while if you enjoy investigative tasks, there are opportunities to train for careers in anti-money laundering, compliance or financial crime prevention.

Salaries vary according to the job and area in which you work. In general, starting salaries are around £11,000 and include a range of benefits such as cheap mortgages, insurance and banking. Once you are trained, pay levels can rise quickly depending on skill and aptitude.

SELF-EMPLOYMENT

There are entry level opportunities for self-employment but they are less common. To stand a good chance of being successful you do need some experience as well as an ability to identify an opportunity. There are many people offering secretarial and typing services from home, acting as part-time or temporary secretaries to different people. Sometimes there are opportunities to specialise, for example in agriculture. Many people have set up successful businesses as farm secretaries responsible for the administration of several farms within a district. There are no set income levels when you are self-employed – it depends entirely on the hours you work, the time involved, the area, the job and the rates you can negotiate.

Commitment, drive, perseverance and support from family and friends help tremendously in ensuring the success path of a business idea into a viable career, but you do need to be totally honest about your skills, knowledge and financial status from the very beginning.

APPRENTICESHIPS

Apprenticeships are widely available, particularly within local government, financial services and major companies. Availability can depend on local employment conditions. It provides a means by which you can earn while you train for a specific career opportunity such as an administrator, a financial advisor, insurance or banking.

For more detailed information about apprenticeships see Chapter 9.

WORKING CONDITIONS

The majority of people working in business, administration and finance are based in offices. They usually spend much of their time working on computers, phones and other office equipment. They will also take part in meetings with colleagues and other businesses either in the same premises or elsewhere. Work environments vary considerably depending on the type of business involved. It may be an old historic house, a small building adjacent to a factory or it could be a modern open plan office, a skyscraper or an isolated farm. You may have an office to yourself, or you may be sharing with many other people.

Working hours tend to be fairly standard across the sector with employees working between 37 and 40 hours a week. Most employees work office hours Monday to Friday. Although 9 am to 5 pm with an hour for lunch is the most common, it is possible to have working hours ranging between 8am and 6pm. Much depends on company policy, and whether or not flexitime is allowed. If flexitime is possible, you would have a requirement to work a set number of hours and be expected to be on the premises within certain periods, but would have the flexibility of starting earlier and finishing later if you wanted. Sometimes it allows you to work longer hours for several days in order to take time off on other occasions if this is acceptable to your employer. Overtime may be required from time to time. This is particularly common in jobs within sales and marketing departments, in secretarial work or when businesses have extra demands on their time such as the end of a financial year. Such overtime is rarely paid for. As we are in a 24/7 society there is an increasing demand from employers in all sectors for people to work shifts, evenings and weekends. 9 am to 5 pm weekdays only, is fast becoming history.

Most companies do not expect you to wear a uniform when working in an office or business environment. You will be able to wear your own clothes but will be expected to dress in a smart, businesslike manner. All companies have their own dress code, and this will vary from business to business. How smart or casual you have to be will depend on your role and the type of business. Many organisations where you will be seen by customers or others will require you to always have smart business dress. But if your role is behind the scenes, the clothing code may be less strict.

Pay levels vary considerably depending on the job chosen, and the sector in which you are working. There may also be perks. A secretary working for a retail business will usually be given a discount on purchases made from the company's shops. Working for a travel company may include discounts on travel arranged through that company. This could involve cheap flights or cheap holidays. Banking and finance organisations may offer low cost insurance and/or mortgages.

BEGINNING A CAREER

Entering the sector can be undertaken at all levels no matter what your educational background. There are opportunities for those with few if any formal qualifications as well as those with degrees. All prospective employees in business, administration and finance are expected to have a reasonable level of literacy and numeracy. Many employers ask for GCSEs in English and Mathematics as a minimum requirement. Office skills such as using computers, touch typing and shorthand are also frequently sought, and many roles require some experience. Often this can be obtained through work experience or by undertaking specialist courses at college to acquire the necessary skills. Higher level roles, such as personal assistants in large companies, are frequently confined to graduates.

No matter what the job, the key skills are always the same. Employers want people who are confident using computers and able to utilise a wide range of software packages. Good communication skills, an ability to get on with all kinds of people, patience and organisational ability are essential. Many jobs require both an ability to work in a team as well as on your own, and customer service skills may be required.

There are always induction courses for new entrants so as to ensure they know how to operate the equipment within the office and to obtain an idea as to how a specific business operates. Further on-the-job training is provided as required. Larger companies and organisations will have a regular appraisal procedure allowing training needs to be highlighted. In smaller companies you may be expected to identify your own training needs: whether it is to go on a first aid course, operate a new software package, assertiveness training or how to manage your time more effectively.

CAREER DEVELOPMENT

The business, finance and administration sector offers good prospects for career development. Structured career paths are rare. Instead, career development often involves taking on extra responsibilities and managing people or projects, or by widening the skills you possess. Many people progress by changing jobs either within the organisation or by taking up employment opportunities within other companies. Getting experience of a range of different roles and different organisations is fast becoming crucial for anyone wanting a senior management post. Legal and other demands on companies mean that they have to be run by people with a wide experience of business. Although it is still possible to climb the ladder just within one company, this is becoming very rare. If you show an aptitude for a specific area of business such as marketing, it may be possible to move into a more specialised role such as a marketing assistant or into management training. Pay levels will reflect your level of experience and skill.

For those able to be flexible about their work and to take opportunities as they arise, the business, administration and finance sector is one which offers considerable potential. It is a sector which is constantly changing and evolving. Some jobs disappear, but others take their place.

DID YOU KNOW?

When the World Wide Web was released in 1991, it had to be dialled up via telephones. It was slow and cumbersome. Within a decade, broadband was creating almost instantaneous connections. Businesses use the internet to promote and sell products, while some companies operate only via the internet.

Thirty years ago, offices were dominated by typewriters and accounting machines. Armies of clerks kept handwritten records of all kinds. Secretaries and copy typists spent hours typing out correspondence and reports. There were even typing pools where a large number of typists worked and a supervisor handed out work as it arrived from elsewhere in the building. The advent of computers on every desk changed this forever. Most managers are now capable of undertaking their own basic correspondence, leaving secretaries to do more advanced work. Clerk typists have been replaced by computer operators working all kinds of different systems. The growth of technology is likely to continue to offer lots of new career opportunities and new working areas in years to come.

Flexibility and a willingness to learn and take on new roles will open many new opportunities.

OPPORTUNITIES FOR TRAVEL

Opportunities for travel depend entirely on the job. Travel may form part of your normal duties, for example a secretary may be required to accompany managers on visits. Also, managers and administrators may be required to visit clients and suppliers, or take part in conferences and exhibitions at a variety of locations throughout the UK. Overseas travel may also be required. If you are working for the European Union, an international company, or a company with offices in more than one country your job may require time to be spent at different offices.

Administrative skills offer considerable opportunities for travel. Such skills are easily transferable and can be used almost anywhere. There are jobs available for secretaries, assistants, administrators and finance clerks in travel organisations, on board ships, with airlines and at outdoor activity centres, to name but a few. For example, at PGL – a market leader in residential activity holidays with centres in the Mediterranean as well as within the UK – centre administrators are vital to the smooth running of each centre. The administrator is responsible for organising accounts, dealing with suppliers and day to day running of the office as well as providing first aid cover and perhaps acting as a duty manager. Skilled personnel within the public sector can apply for positions with European Union institutions including the European Commission.

Opportunities for working overseas will depend a great deal on the country involved. Unless it is an English speaking country such as the United States of America, South Africa or New Zealand, you will almost certainly require some knowledge of the national language being spoken. Bilingual secretaries and administrators are always in demand and can command quite high salaries.

CHAPTER 5
CASE STUDY 1

CLARE CHILDERLEY

National Trust Administrator

Clare Childerley works for the National Trust as administrator
of Wimpole Hall in Cambridgeshire. Her career to date has been
quite varied revealing the flexibility of her administrative skills.

'When I left school I wanted to work in business and administration.
I felt that it would give me a steady job and a good income. I went
to college to do a BTEC national diploma in Business and Finance,
then obtained a Higher Diploma in Administrative Procedures. This
gave me a good business grounding.

'My first job was with the RSPB (Royal Society for the Protection
of Birds) where I worked as administrator to the direct mail team.
This involved dealing with appeals, making sure that all the proofs
for each mailing were sent to the right people, administering the
raffle in *Birds* magazine as well as undertaking general secretarial
and administrative jobs.

'I then moved to CamVet – the Cambridge University Veterinary
School Trust – as appeals administrator. I was involved with
organising the Friends Open Day, regular meetings and get-
togethers, monitoring the income for appeals as well as keeping
databases up to date. It was quite a varied job.

'After this I had a complete change and went to work at a construction company, Amey Building, where I was Personal Assistant to the Marketing Manager. I provided secretarial back up as well as helping to prepare presentations to prospective clients and organise corporate hospitality days. My job ended abruptly when I was made redundant.

'I took the first job I was offered. This was at a company providing a medical writing service to pharmaceutical companies. I had to write up reports and provide secretarial services to four doctors. This was not the most interesting job that I have had. I stuck it out for a year as it would not have been good for my CV to move on too quickly.

'My next job was at Novartis Animal Health working in sales and marketing. This was really interesting and challenging. I was providing secretarial services to 15 representatives. I helped organise roadshows, product launches, conferences, meetings and was responsible for ordering stock for the free-of-charge sample cupboards. When we launched new products there were incentives for veterinary practices to use the products. If they bought so many of our products, they would get free equipment in return. It was my job to organise and source the equipment they requested. This job involved a lot of travel, with product launches held in places like Barcelona and Marrakesh.

'The job came to an end when the company was relocated. I had the choice of relocating to Frimley or taking redundancy. As I did not want to leave the area, I chose redundancy. This time, I took longer to find a new job as I wanted to make sure I made the right decision.

'This was when I started working at Wimpole Hall and I have not regretted it. The job is really interesting. As administrator I have a lot of responsibility. I am responsible for group bookings, ensuring that all paperwork is correct and everyone is informed. I deal with all incoming phone calls including enquiries about the property and the various events held here. I take bookings for tickets, and update all voice mail messages, organise data to be submitted to head office, supervise volunteer office staff and ensure they have plenty of work to do. A key part of my job is to send out a programme to everyone on the estate so that they know what is happening, which groups are visiting and what activities are being planned during the week. In addition, I provide assistance wherever it is needed on the estate.

'I have been here two years now and really enjoy it. It is very varied and there is never a dull moment.

'Working in as many offices as I have done has shown me how transferable my skills are. You can be general or work in a very specialised area and still use the same skills. All offices are based upon operational systems, all you have to do is learn those systems. You have to be very diplomatic, and try to get on with everyone. Politeness is essential and it is important to treat everyone the same way. Listen and learn and do the work the way they want you to. In every job there have been lots of opportunities to take training courses. It is important to keep up-to-date with business methods. Courses I have attended include negotiating skills, how to prioritise, using time effectively, communication skills, health and safety, first aid, assertiveness training and of course computer training.

'I enjoy my job and have no plans to move on.'

CHAPTER 6
TOOLS OF THE TRADE

Having decided that a career in business, finance and administration is for you, the big question that has to be asked is: 'Do you have the personal qualities that are needed to make a successful career?'

No matter what the job, everyone involved in business, finance and administration shares certain key characteristics. An interest in the subject is obviously essential – you wouldn't want to spend the rest of your life doing something that bores you silly or that you really dislike. Remember that you may be spending up to 10 hours a day at work in the same environment.

You also need to be able to keep things confidential. Working in any form of administration means that you will have access to files which can contain sensitive information, perhaps on people if working in a human resources department, to the financial well being of the company, or even to the country as a whole. In some sectors of government you may be asked to sign the Official Secrets Act.

Equally important is an ability to get on with everyone. Good communication skills are extremely important if you are working in a customer service, secretarial or administrative role involving the public. You may find people you encounter are bad tempered, unhappy or angry. A calm attitude and a willingness to deal with anyone on the same terms is essential. Even if you do not like someone, you still have to work with them and to deal with them on a day to day basis. Being on good terms with your work colleagues makes for a much more pleasant work environment.

Other key personal qualities are patience, reliability, common sense and an ability to prioritise tasks.

- ▶ You must be able to cope under pressure. There will be times in every office when the workload is especially heavy, and you have to be able to cope without panicking. Accuracy and attention to detail are important.

- ▶ You need to be a good time keeper. Meetings and conferences have to start on time and not overrun. Offices will need to open on time with all staff present.

- ▶ You may be required to juggle a variety of tasks such as arranging a meeting, writing a report and conducting business negotiations, as well as dealing with phone calls and emails. You must be prepared to undertake repetitive tasks such as a type of letter which has to be sent out again and again, or being responsible for ordering supplies.

- ▶ You need to be confident yet willing to listen to other people's point of view and alter what you are doing when necessary. Dealing with the public, colleagues and other organisations in person, by phone and email will be required on a daily basis.

UNLIKELY START

Business ideas often come from the most unlikely places. We all take frozen food for granted. From frozen vegetables to ready meals, it is a multi-million pound industry. Yet it all came about as a result of a chance visit made by a man called Clarence Birdseye in 1912. On a visit to Newfoundland, Canada, he saw people left fish outside to keep fresh as it was so cold. Struck by the idea, Clarence Birdseye went home and invented a machine that would quick freeze all kinds of foods. His name lives on – Birds Eye is a well known name on the supermarket freezer shelves.

OUTSIDE INFLUENCES

Businesses can be affected by factors outside their control. The terrorist attacks on New York and Washington in 2001 and the subsequent military action in Afghanistan had a major impact on businesses all over the world. People avoided flying so airlines lost money. The stock market fell dramatically wiping millions of pounds off shares in all businesses as people sold shares fearing they would lose their money if they did not.

Smaller companies will expect you to be flexible in what you do. As well as undertaking a variety of roles within your job you may be expected to help in other roles when times are busy or people are sick. The larger the organisation, the more inflexible your role is likely to be. In many government jobs you will be restricted to a specific role with very little flexibility of how you do it, and with a much more rigid structure of supervision and management than you get in the private sector.

If you are working in the public sector, you will be required to carry out policies that are decided by central and/or local government. These may be something that you personally disagree with. You are not allowed to show either your agreement or disagreement with agreed policies, either with colleagues or the public. This can be constricting. A change of control at central or local level can not only change a policy, but change how it is implemented. A change may mean a total reversal of what you were doing. So throughout your career you could find there are things you agree with

DID YOU KNOW?

The nickname for a Japanese business employee is 'Salaryman'.

and things that you do not agree with. You personally are not allowed to change policy or how it is implemented. If you have strong political views of any kind, working in the public sector is probably not for you.

Working in the financial sector will require good mathematical skills. Financial information will need to be prepared and you will need to be happy working with figures for much of the day. Some jobs will be almost completely devoted to figure work such as in accountancy. Problem solving and managerial skills are also needed.

It is well worth looking closely at your own character and existing skills to see if you match these requirements. Look for examples in your daily life to show that you can be reliable, confident and can deal with people. If you are hesitant about any of these qualities seek the advice of your friends, teachers and other people who know you well. Do they believe you have the necessary qualities to work in business, administration and finance? Can they suggest any examples of your work or personal character which show those qualities in practice?

Most employers expect staff to have at least English and Maths GCSEs. It is important to be able to write clearly and be a good communicator both in speech and writing. Every office job will require some use of mathematics, ranging from keeping accounts to organising finances for meetings and conferences.

Work experience will enable you to discover what life is like in a business sector. It enables you to develop skills such as administration, communication and organisation as well as gaining some specialist knowledge. Contact local companies, organisations and local government to see if they can offer work placements. Say what type of skills you have and what you are interested in doing. They may also be able to offer work shadowing schemes where you can follow someone through their daily work, seeing just what a particular job offers as a career. Such opportunities are worth taking as they enable you to gain detailed knowledge and to talk to people about their jobs on a one to one basis.

Work experience will also enable you to give prospective employers contact with people who can provide independent references as to your work ability. Always check with prospective referees first to ensure they are happy for you to give their names as references.

If you are involved with a charity or organisation in your spare time, whether it be the Scouts or a drama club, offer to help with the organisation and administration. Again, this will provide useful experience that can be referred to when going for interviews.

SELF-EMPLOYMENT

If you are aiming for self-employment or setting up your own business from the beginning, you need to make sure you have done all your research and sought all the help required. You need to be totally honest with yourself – and with any prospective investors – as to your commitment, desire to succeed, financial status and the personal qualities you can bring to a business. Seek help from organisations such as www.businesslink.gov.uk which has an extremely useful guide covering aspects like market research, financial commitment, business skills, product development, sales and marketing skills.

Shell LiveWIRE is another useful site for young people seeking to obtain the necessary tools and advice to set up businesses. It is the UK's biggest online community for young entrepreneurs,

BUSINESS NAMES

Many business names are specially created. Amtrak is a combination of the words American and Track while Sony was originally called Totsucken, but the company felt that this would be difficult to pronounce. The name Sony was invented as a cross between sound, sonic and sonny. Sonny was felt to represent a young man or boy thus showing an energetic young company, and would also link into the concept of sound. Thus Sony was born.

BUSINESS JARGON

Business jargon is all too common. Some have become extremely well known such as Murphy's Law. This states: 'Anything that can go wrong will go wrong.' If there is more than one possible outcome of a task, and one of those outcomes results in disaster then someone will inevitably choose to do it that way. Another example is K.I.S.S., which stands for KEEP IT SIMPLE, STUPID! This refers to the obvious approach being the best. Whether it is organising a conference, designing a product, arranging a meeting – keep everything as simple as possible. That way there is less chance of anything going wrong.

providing help and advice within a discussion forum, a business library as well as the opportunity to win money for investment. Typical of award winners is Luke Jefferson, co-founder of Scratchface – a start up company which has developed an innovative Huetility device which helps decode colours for the colour blind. The £1,000 cash injection from Shell LiveWIRE provided funds to develop a new application of this technology for the iPhone. Luke says:

> 'It is more important than ever to be really canny about your target market. As a young entrepreneur, the key thing is to have belief in your business idea, remain confident and press on. We're targeting our Huetility product to the hugely popular iPhone applications market and at buyers who we believe will be relatively unaffected by the recession. As a start-up we've become used to living modestly and surviving on a low wage, so there's a sense in which we could be taking this step in any economic environment. We'll keep going with this, no matter what our or the country's economic circumstances are like. We're determined to make a success of our business.'

Millionaire Gill Fielding is involved with the Wealth Intelligence Academy and recommends that young people considering setting up their own business should do their preparation first. She says, 'Practise with somebody successful. Get a mentor and a coach. Get connected with people that will support and motivate you – network. Get access to people, networks and clubs where the people who may have answers for you will go. Go and look at businesses successfully doing what you want to do – what can you learn? Go and be a customer and experience their product or service – what did you like and what not? Can you improve on their service? Research the customer and the other providers in the market place.'

CHAPTER 7
FAQs

What are the key considerations to bear in mind if opting for a job in this sector?

 How do you know if it will suit you?

You need to be well organised, methodical and enjoy office work. Using computers is essential and good keyboard skills are also essential for any administrative or secretarial position. Numeracy is important. Most jobs will need a reasonable skill in figure work and keeping accounts. You need to be self-motivated and able to get on with the job without being continually supervised. Anyone working in business or the financial sector in whatever capacity has to be able to accept responsibility for their work. Depending on the job, you may need to be able to work on your own or in a team. Politeness and discretion are essential as is an ability to keep secrets. Working in any aspect of business or administration means you may be responsible for staff records or sensitive business information. Honesty is important – particularly if you are working in any aspect of finance. You may be dealing with very large sums of money.

 How much will I get paid?

Salaries vary from job to job and even identical jobs in different organisations can have a wide range of salaries. There are no national or business sector benchmarks; much depends on how easy it is for companies to get staff. In general expect a starting salary of around £10,000 depending on skills and qualifications. This increases as you become more experienced. Senior positions, for example secretaries or administrators, can result in salaries of £22,000 or more. Managerial positions can be in excess of £30,000. Depending on the company for which you are working there may well be other benefits such as cheap travel, insurance, mortgages.

What hours will I have to work?

Office hours are generally from 9am until 5pm with an hour for lunch. This can vary slightly depending on company requirements starting perhaps at 8am and ending at 4pm, or starting at 10am and ending at 6pm. Some organisations operate a flexitime policy. This is where you are required to be in the office for a certain number of hours each day or each week. You can adjust these hours to suit your needs. For example, one day you may need to have time off for a dentist appointment, so you could make up the time by coming in earlier or staying later on a different day. Overtime may be required from time to time and this could involve occasional evening or even weekend work. This is usually unpaid. Once some experience is obtained, it can be possible to work on a temporary basis for various office agencies who supply staff on demand to a variety of companies. This can involve moving frequently from company to company, and working a variety of hours. This can be a good way of gaining experience in different sectors and different areas of work to see what suits you best.

Are there any apprenticeships available?

Apprenticeships are available in both administration and the financial services sectors. They are open to people aged 16 and above and provide a mixture of on- and off-the-job training. It involves working alongside experienced staff in a real job to gain job specific skills and experience. In addition you would undertake training at college to gain professional qualifications.

What opportunities are there?

The opportunities are endless. A good administrator or secretary is rarely out of work – there are always new work opportunities arising. Every company and organisation require administrators, secretaries and finance staff. Business, finance and administrative skills are easily transferable. Once you have some basic experience, it is easy to take those skills into other sectors although if you want to specialise it is possible to do so. Medical and legal work often require specialists, as do accountants and financial operations.

Where will I work?

For much of the time you will be working in an office. Depending on the job and the location, you may be required to travel, or to supervise activities elsewhere on site. You will normally be working for two or three people or, once you are more experienced, you could be working on your own and responsible for the daily operation of an office.

How could my career progress?

This will depend very much on the industry sector in which you are working, and the type of work being undertaken. There are no clear structured career paths. Generally people take on extra responsibilities, learning to manage projects or by gaining new skills. Many people progress their careers by moving from company to company, gaining experience and taking on more varied roles. If you have an interest in a particular type of activity, for example legal work, it is possible to obtain qualifications enabling you to move into pure administrative roles. It is possible to use a general business, administrative or financial role as a way of entering management positions in functions such as marketing, public relations, finance, or local government.

What are the opportunities for travel?

Since business and administrative skills are easily transferable, it is easy to move to another area of the country and find work. International companies may provide opportunities to work in other countries, although this may involve learning another language. Business, finance and administrative staff are needed on cruise ships and in travel related organisations. Depending on your job, you may be required to travel as part of your work providing administrative back up at conferences, product launches, presentations and meetings.

Q **How can I increase the chances of success in self-employment or setting up a business?**

A You need enthusiasm, persistence, an ability to work hard, organisational skills, a willingness to take risks, business knowledge and good communication skills as well as a lot of patience. Take advantage of all the business courses and advice on offer from organisations like The Prince's Trust. Keep a close control over finances.

Q **Is there a structured career progression?**

A As this is a wide ranging sector, there are no clear cut career structures. Even within a specialist role in a specialist sub-sector, there is no career structure. Most businesses have now done away with any structure, as the world moves at too fast a pace for these to mean anything.

Q **Do financial services have career structures?**

A Sadly no. There is no overall structure as there are three main streams, i.e. insurance, banking and finance within each of which there is a wide range of specialist areas, all of which need different skills and qualifications. As well as a wide variety of professional associations each offering a wide range of qualifications, many banks and insurers have their own in-house schemes. One of the reasons that there is no structure is that within the sector there is such a wide range of businesses and jobs. Although there are three mainstream areas, individual businesses can straddle all three, as can individual jobs, e.g. an accountant in an insurance company owned by a bank.

BUSINESS MYTHS

Listed below are some typical myths surrounding starting and running a business that have been proved wrong by Department of Trade and Industry research.

Myth: It takes years to start a business from scratch.

Fact: Most businesses are established within six months.

Myth: The rejection figure for business loan applications is very high.

Fact: Overall, only 10–20% of applications are rejected.

Myth: It is difficult to make an adequate living from a new business.

Fact: People's estimate of income in their first year of trading is only half of the figure actually achieved by small businesses.

CHAPTER 8
CASE STUDY 2

BECKY NEWBERRY

Assistant Administrator, Human Resources

Nineteen year old Becky Newberry did not expect to work in administration after leaving school but has found it extremely interesting. She now works for PGL Travel Ltd, the UK's leading provider of residential activity holidays for children.

'I started studying for A levels but found this path just wasn't for me. I made the decision to leave education and found a job working in a local pub. I soon found myself out of work again as the pub cut my shifts due to a lack of trade. While I was unemployed I was trying hard to get a job. I didn't really have any formal working experience – I could use a computer but I believe my lack of job experience was making it hard for me to get an interview.

'I attended a recruitment fair at Ryde Job Centre where I met representatives from PGL Travel Ltd. I chatted to Chrissy George, the Human Resources Supervisor at PGL's Little Canada Activity Centre, and took an application form away. I subsequently applied and was successful.

'Working in the office at PGL has given me the chance to develop my administration experience and learn new skills.

I am now Assistant Administrator in Human Resources. I have to communicate with head office and staff at the Little Canada Activity Centre. It is a good job to have.

'My job involves general administrative work including lots of spreadsheets, making posters for events, distributing staff uniforms and being in charge of the payroll, which I really enjoy. Everyone's nice and welcoming and there's a good range of people here. Lots of the seasonal staff are a similar age to me and my role is diverse; every day I could do something different. I've since learned that there were sixty applicants for my job, with ten making it through to an interview.

'Working here has given me valuable experience and I have learned a lot of skills. It was easy to learn the work as I had a lot of on-the-job training, especially from my boss.

'Within six weeks of taking up this job, I had gained a First Aid Course Certificate. I want to get as many qualifications as I can through PGL – the Apprenticeship in Customer Service is my next aim. This will enable me to gain an NVQ in customer service. As part of the course I have to gain experience in all the different functions within the centre. This course will take about a year to complete.'

CHAPTER 9
QUALIFICATIONS AND TRAINING

There is a wide range of business qualifications that can be obtained at school or college which will enable you to gain basic skills and practical knowledge to progress in a career within business, finance and administration.

DIPLOMA IN BUSINESS, ADMINISTRATION AND FINANCE

The Diploma in Business, Administration and Finance is designed to provide you with a solid grounding in up-to-the-minute business skills. It is a way of developing an understanding of what business is all about and how it works in practice. Among the many skills it teaches are how to plan and manage personal finances, flexibility, team working, communication and self-motivation. The diploma has been created to meet the requirements of employers in business enterprise, business administration, personal finance and financial services, customer service, sales and business communication.

At Foundation level you will:

▶ investigate different types of products and services
▶ understand the main administrative roles and processes that support business
▶ acquire the skills necessary to manage personal finance and spending
▶ explore different communication methods
▶ develop skills in dealing with other people
▶ have an introduction to basic selling techniques.

At Higher level you will:

▶ learn how innovation and creativity benefit business
▶ develop the communication skills required by business
▶ learn more about personal finance and financial services
▶ explore marketing and sales
▶ find out how business interacts with the local, national and global community.

At Advanced level you will:

▶ explore theories of communication and how they are practised
▶ research financial products and services
▶ study business taxation, costing, budgetry planning and control
▶ investigate how marketing is used to increase demand for products and services
▶ learn how to handle customers in a business environment
▶ investigate corporate social responsibility.

GCSEs

GCSE qualifications are available in business studies, applied business, business subjects and economics. The content varies according to the type of course, but generally covers topics such as the legal and financial aspects of starting and developing business, how finance is raised and used by governments and businesses, practical applications of business and economics, simple accounting, cash flow forecasting, marketing, and basic management techniques.

BTEC AND OCR NATIONAL AWARDS

There is a range of BTEC awards relating to careers in business, finance and administration. These qualifications offer a mix of theory and practice and often include an element of work experience. They can form part of an apprenticeship course.

BTEC National Diploma in Business

This is a 2 year course and covers a range of subjects.

Core modules are: business structures and goals, business environment, marketing processes, physical resources, human resources, administrative systems, innovation and change, information systems, international marketing systems, accounting procedures, quantitative methods, and behaviour at work. An extra subject from small business computer systems, advertising, international trade, personnel policies and practice or business law must be chosen.

There is also a BTEC National Award in Personal and Business Finance covering core units in financial services for individuals, business financial performance, financial services to support business, and financial services regulation ethics and trends. In addition, two specialist units have to be completed from a selection of topics including finance in the national economy, finance in the global economy, preparing for employment, and exploring computer applications for financial management.

On completion of such courses, it is possible to pass on to BTEC Higher National qualifications such as the BTEC HND in Business (Finance) or foundation degrees.

BTEC HND in Business (Finance) requires you to study eight core units:

1. business decision making
2. marketing
3. managing financial resources and decisions
4. organisations and behaviour
5. business environment
6. common law
7. business strategy
8. research project.

Four compulsory specialist units:

1. management accounting costing and budgeting
2. financial systems and auditing
3. financial reporting
4. taxation.

Plus four specialist units. These have to be chosen from a long list of topics. Typical options include:

- marketing intelligence
- human resources development
- English legal system
- marketing planning
- managing activities to achieve results.

The Edxcel website contains a full list of options.

The OCR Nationals in Business, Information Technology and Public Services cover all forms of business including retail, human resources, finance, law, sales and marking and administration. There is also a Certificate in Employability Skills dealing with areas such as personal effectiveness and success at work, developing personal communication skills, developing team skills and positive working relationships, health, safety and security in the workplace. Qualifications range from level 1 to level 3 awards.

City & Guilds offers a Level 1 Certificate in Book Keeping and Accounts as well as a Certificate in Computerised Accounts. City & Guilds also offers a NVQ in Business and Administration. This

---

EMBARRASSING BUSINESS

Three of the most embarrassing business mistakes ever made:

1. Doing a Ratner has become a famous business phrase. Gerald Ratner was owner of a large chain of jewellery stores. Talking to journalists he went on record saying that the earrings he sold were rubbish and 'cheaper than a Marks & Spencer prawn sandwich but probably wouldn't last as long'. His business collapsed almost overnight as shoppers refused to buy his products.
2. In 1985, Coca-Cola scrapped the traditional Coke formula in favour of a sweeter 'New Coke' drink. Sales dropped dramatically as consumers complained about the flavour change. When executives finally admitted their mistake and reintroduced the original formula coke sales rose – and new Coke quietly disappeared from the shelves.
3. McDonald's Japan sought to improve business by giving away 10,000 MP3 players branded with their logo. Unfortunately the promotion backfired. The players contained a virus which when let loose on hard drives, forwarded usernames and passwords to a network of online hackers.

is a modular award allowing you to study a variety of subjects relating to business and administration, customer service, and management, depending on whether you are aiming for a level 2 or level 3 award.

WORK BASED TRAINING

Once in work, you will receive induction training into the systems and organisation of the company. Further training will be provided on the job as required. Often this may be gained by working alongside employees undertaking similar work. Larger companies will normally provide in-house courses, as well as the opportunity to participate in external courses run by colleges and other organisations. There are many extra training opportunities that can be taken which are relevant to careers in this sector such as customer service training, supervisory training, first aid, fund raising and appeals management.

In smaller businesses you may have to identify your own training needs and seek permission to attend the relevant courses. This could range from courses dealing with various software package operations, customer service, time management or finance skills.

It is possible to study for additional business related qualifications which will benefit career development. These qualifications can range from NVQs and SVQs at levels 1 to 4, HNC and HND, business diplomas to foundation degrees. Most of these courses are generally studied at college on a full-time or part-time basis or through online open learning networks. It may require you to study in the evenings or at weekends, although some companies may give time off to attend classes. Qualifications such as these generally involve workshops, lectures and assignments based on workplace tasks, together with an end of qualification knowledge based test.

NVQs are work based qualifications and assessment generally takes place in the workplace. There are five levels ranging from routine competencies to complex, professional or technical work activities at level 5. They are not time limited or age restricted.

A qualification in business and administration can enable you to specialise in different areas such as human resources, legal or medical sectors. Specialist qualifications can be obtained relating to jobs like medical or legal secretaries, legal assistants, personnel administration, recruitment advisors or as a professional fund raiser.

There are numerous useful skills such as touch typing, shorthand, and first aid qualifications which can be obtained via short external courses at any stage in your career.

FINANCIAL SERVICES

There are numerous specialist awards, certificates and diplomas which can be obtained in the various branches of financial services. These are offered by organisations such as the Chartered Insurance Institute, the Institute of Banking and the IFS School of Finance. Such specialist qualifications are essential for anyone planning to develop a career in any aspect of the financial services.

Awards

Awards have no formal entry requirements. The Award in Insurance aims to develop an understanding of key insurance issues including:

- ▶ how the insurance market operates
- ▶ fundamental risk and insurance principles and procedures
- ▶ core personal and commercial insurance products.

The Award in Financial Planning aims to provide a solid grounding in core financial and life assurance products. It offers guidance on sound professional practice.

Certificates

Certificates require more detailed study of a chosen branch of the financial services sector. For example, the Certificate in Mortgage Advice is aimed at those intending to become mortgage advisors or to work in a support role while the Certificate in Financial Administration is essential for anyone looking for a financial service career in administration, customer support, compliance and technical guidance.

The Certificate in Financial Administration provides a thorough grounding in:

▶ the financial services industry, including key aspects of legislation and regulation, and helps develop an appreciation of the process of investment planning and the types of products involved

▶ the administration of life or pensions business depending on the unit selected.

The Certificate in Financial Planning focuses on:

▶ the operation of the financial services market
▶ financial planning advice
▶ regulatory issues
▶ the mechanics and purpose of the main investment products
▶ the process of giving advice to clients.

The Certificate in Insurance is a core qualification for all staff working across all areas of the industry and is a logical progression from a foundation award. It provides a grounding in:

▶ basic insurance principles including the regulatory environment
▶ the key insurance disciplines of underwriting and claims
▶ popular products including motor, household, healthcare and packaged commercial insurances.

For further information about where you can apply to take these qualifications please see Chapter 12.

Diplomas

Typical of the diplomas available are the Professional Diploma in Financial Services Management, the Applied Diploma in Corporate Banking, and the Applied Diploma in Risk and Insurance Management. These qualifications are designed to equip you with a sound understanding of the principles involved, and to study how those principles are applied in business life. They tend to be a higher grade than the certificates. For example, the Diploma in Financial Planning develops advanced knowledge and understanding of:

- personal taxation
- trusts
- business planning
- pension funding
- pension income
- investment
- supervision in a regulated environment
- financial planning practice.

The majority of these qualifications are generally obtained by completing modules on a distance learning basis. Examinations can generally be taken online, enabling you to take the exam when you are ready. These diplomas can act as a stepping stone to higher professional qualifications.

Within financial services there are literally hundreds of different qualifications below the level of degree or full professional qualification. A full professional qualification in insurance or banking will enable you to work anywhere within those sectors. Nowadays, these are at first or second degree level. The wide range of qualifications and awards below these top levels will only be relevant to work in a specific sector, e.g. mortgage finance. Below that, award levels are frequently only relevant to the particular job and/or employer; they are rarely recognised elsewhere in the sector.

The regulators of financial services are introducing new qualification requirements some time soon after 2009. The Retail Distribution Review seeks to move from the current exam regime for advisors, which is roughly equivalent to A level standard, to a higher level 4 standard which is between A level and first year undergraduate level, but the Financial Services Skills Council list of relevant qualifications has a full 13 pages just listing the titles of qualifications for financial advisors between levels 1 and 8.

To gain professional status within the financial sector you will need to obtain recognised qualifications. To be an accountant for example, you can gain qualifications from the Association of Chartered Certified Accountants. At the lowest level there is the Certified Accounting Technician (CAT) which requires you to complete nine exams and undertake one year's practical experience. Obtaining the CAT qualification gives exemption from three out of 14 papers required for the ACCA qualification to become a fully qualified accountant.

To take another example, that of insurance, a typical non-degree career path could lead through a range of specialist qualifications: Certificate in Insurance, Diploma in Insurance, Advanced Diploma in Insurance, and Chartered Status. Exams have to be taken at each stage.

APPRENTICESHIPS

A range of apprenticeships are available including:

▶ Apprenticeship in Administration
▶ Apprenticeship in Retail Financial Services

▶ Advanced Apprenticeship in Advising on Financial Products
▶ Apprenticeship and Advanced Apprenticeship in Retail Financial Services (Retail Banking and General Insurance)
▶ Apprenticeship and Advanced Apprenticeship in Accounting
▶ Apprenticeship and Advanced Apprenticeship in Payroll
▶ Modern Apprenticeship in Accounting
▶ Modern Apprenticeship in Providing Financial Services.

Apprenticeships have been developed for a wide range of industry sectors. There are 180 career choices in 80 industry sectors. In the business administration and law sector, apprenticeships include:

▶ accounting
▶ business and administration
▶ advising on financial products
▶ providing financial services
▶ payroll.

What you do daily will depend on the sector, the apprenticeship, the employer, and your individual role.

During an apprenticeship you would gain practical experience in your chosen work area, for example as an accounting apprentice you might be keeping track of a specific finance account. As a business and administration apprentice you might be typing, putting financial information on spreadsheets, dealing with the post, and photocopying. In addition, you would undertake day release courses at local colleges.

All employed apprentices must receive a wage of no less than £95 per week, but government research says that apprentices on average earn £170 per week.

The length of time needed to complete an apprenticeship depends on the subject, the ability of the apprentice, previous knowledge and specific requirements of the employer. In general, an apprenticeship will usually take around 12–18 months to complete and an advanced apprenticeship around 24 months.

To find out if there is an apprenticeship place available in your area you can apply online via www.apprenticeshipsonline.org. In England you can contact your local Connexions/Careers Office or go to www.apprenticeships.org.uk. In Scotland advice on local colleges and providers who offer apprenticeships can be found via Skills Development Scotland www.skillsdevelopmentsscotland. co.uk or www.modernapprenticeships.com. In Wales go to www. careerswales.com. The DECYP and Careers Wales Advisors can provide advice on colleges and providers and may be able to help with finding a local employer. In Northern Ireland DELNI www. delni.gov.uk/index/successthroughskills/apprenticeshipshipsni. htm and Careers Northern Ireland www.careersserviceni.com will be able to help. Alternatively if you have a potential employer in mind, you can contact them to see if they will train you via the apprenticeship programme.

OLD TIMERS

Some companies date back centuries. John Brooke and Sons Ltd is thought to be the oldest surviving family business in the UK. The company was founded as a wool cloth mill in 1541 by the Brooke family. The mills now house a Heritage Office Park. Whitechapel Bell Foundry is Britain's oldest manufacturing company being established in 1570; it is where Big Ben was made. R Durtnell & Sons Ltd is Britain's oldest building company, having been established in 1591, and the first house built by John Durtnell and his brother Brian, for their father in 1593, still stands today.

SELF-EMPLOYMENT AND SETTING UP A BUSINESS

Help and advice can be obtained from a variety of organisations such as The Prince's Trust which has a Business Programme targeting young people aged 18–30 who are living in England, Wales or Northern Ireland and are unemployed or working less than 16 hours a week. You can apply online to join the Business Programme and gain advice on employment options, business skills training, business planning support, start-up funding, and ongoing support from a mentor.

There are also short courses which offer intensive training and experience in a specific sector to help young people get jobs. Over 1,500 businesses graduate each year from the Business Programme.

Valuable advice to would-be entrepreneurs is also to be found in the *Bright Ideas Handbook*, published by *Which?* It provides practical, step by step guidance for understanding intellectual property law and tips on how to find and use the best lawyer, how to make the pitch of a lifetime, plan an advertising and marketing strategy, and how to get distribution of your product or service up and running.

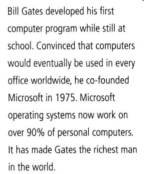

DID YOU KNOW?

Bill Gates developed his first computer program while still at school. Convinced that computers would eventually be used in every office worldwide, he co-founded Microsoft in 1975. Microsoft operating systems now work on over 90% of personal computers. It has made Gates the richest man in the world.

Taking part in young enterprise activities if offered by your school can provide valuable experience and knowledge. Many young people use these activities as a springboard for their future careers.

FIGURE 1
ACCESS TO BUSINESS, ADMINISTRATION
AND FINANCE INDUSTRIES

Including management, self-employment and setting up a business

CHAPTER 10
REAL LIVES

RICHARD SIMMONS

Since leaving school, Richard Simmons has set up his own business
and seen its evolution into a new concept as well as becoming a
Young Ambassador for The Prince's Trust.

'After leaving school at 18, I was having a tough time at home as
my parents were going through a messy divorce. I drifted from
one job to another, mostly in retail but did not feel fulfilled. I had
always been very creative and felt frustrated working behind a till
all day.

'I turned to art to escape my problems. I enjoyed designing
T-shirts and got a batch made up to sell. I was surprised at how
popular they were and decided to launch my own business. I drew
up a comprehensive plan and took it to The Prince's Trust. They
were so impressed with the vision and professional skills that I
received a £2,000 loan within a month. I was put on the Business
Plan, given business training and assigned a mentor. The loan had
to be paid off within two years and I worked with the mentor for a
further year after that.

'After a couple of years I had taken the business as far as I could,
and was bored. I wanted to do more with my art and help people at
the same time. In February 2008, I decided to evolve the business
into something new and launched Art is the Cure. This is a project

which promotes the use of art, as a way of overcoming depression, self-harm and addiction. A lot of people cannot talk about their problems or verbalise their pain so using art in any form as a creative outlet can help people tell their story and get negative emotions out of their system. The aim is to encourage people to pick up a paint brush or play some music to get the release they need rather than picking up a razor blade or turning to drugs or alcohol.

'When doing the London Edge fashion show I managed to sign a labelling deal with an American agent from Los Angeles to do a clothing range to be sold into fashion stores as well as selling online through MySpace.

'I have received hundreds of messages from people all over the world telling me that the project has helped them overcome their problems. Doctors have even been in touch to say they have started referring depressed patients to the website. The project has made a (huge impact on) MySpace and Art is the Cure has the potential to be a global success. The intention is to put on gigs and tours, free art workshops, live painting shows and art auctions to raise the profile of the campaign. I am also in talks with TV producers about doing a documentary.

'In addition, I have become a Young Ambassador for The Prince's Trust and did some courses in leadership and public speaking. This work involves giving talks to schools, businesses and the media about the work of the Trust and how it has helped me set up a business. I am very happy with what I am doing and the next five years look very promising with lots of opportunities opening up.'

ED RIGG

Ed Rigg's career demonstrates how varied business life can be, and how experience in one sector be transferred easily into another.

'I started working straight after school for a film production company as a runner where I worked for three years. I rose through the ranks to work as a production manager and director's assistant. I then moved to Budapest to live and started to direct my own music videos and short films. After returning to the UK I tried to pursue a career as a director but it never materialised and then I started Eager drinks.

'I started Eager drinks because I could not find any decent apple juice in bars in the UK so decided to try and make some that people would buy. The brand was started from my kitchen table and then we went to sell bar to bar. This has grown over the last 3 years and now we sell to well over 500 bars nationally. We have tried to focus on value for money and delivering to the bar industry what it wants, good quality juices that do not need to be refrigerated before being opened. This allows them to reduce their wastage and also reduce the amount of fridge space and increase the convenience when storing the products.

'I would like to think that we can offer the same benefits as we have shown the bar industry to the UK consumer. If fewer people drink concentrated fruit juices and more start buying Eager, and if it makes it easier for people to be healthier and also get great quality juices, then we are doing the right job. We also want people to be greener, and having juices that do not need to be refrigerated really reduces the carbon footprint.

'For the future we are focusing on the core elements of what the brand has to offer but we want to develop the character of the brand and communicate our underlying values. Eager drinks are determined to take on the big multinational brands and prove we can create our own foothold in the marketplace. Eager is breaking away as we are not a fruit juice brand that is too worthy and self-righteous, we just want people to think of Eager as a brand that offers great quality juices with a bit of attitude and determination and a brand that is not afraid to take on the establishment. Eager is not complicated in its honest enthusiasm and in doing the simple things well.

'I would recommend doing an apprenticeship or getting a job if you are not particularly interested in academic studies. It can be great to just go out and get experience. I started my business because I felt I had some experience of business and marketing. Also it's important to head in a direction even if it's not the right one; it will lead to something else. Do not be afraid to fail. Most people do not try things because they are afraid; just be bold and don't worry what people will say if it does not work. Finally, do not be afraid to go back and study even if you think it is too late. It is far better to go and study a subject you are interested in, having found it later in life, and then you can apply your life skills with much more authority.'

CHAPTER 11
THE LAST WORD

Having read this book, you should now have a good idea as to whether a career in business, finance and administration offers you the opportunities you are looking for. For the right person, this is a sector which can offer tremendous job satisfaction and career development.

Some people may still be uncertain. This does not mean that the sector is wrong for you; it just means you need more time to think. This book does not set out to be comprehensive, answering every question you might possibly have about the sector. Instead it aims to give an overview and guidance on what it means to work in business, finance and administration. There is much more that can be learned. Within the sector there is an enormous variety in types of employer, the business they are in, and employee roles. This wide variety may look confusing, but there is a common thread. However big or small, private or public, they all need people to administer the business, answer the phone and talk to customers.

Anyone who is seriously considering a career in this sector should consider trying to obtain some work experience doing the types of job in which you are interested. It is the only way in which you can really find out whether you would be suited to it. Having relevant work experience also looks good on your CV and may also lead to work opportunities. Talk to people already working in the business area you are interested in, find out about their jobs and career development. Seek their advice. They will be only

DID YOU KNOW?
The largest employer in the world is the Indian Railway system which employs over 1.6 million people.

too willing to help. Contact companies in the sectors in which you are interested and find out about career opportunities.

If you are already in work, and looking for a career change, getting work experience is still essential. It will enable you to test out your aptitude and find out if it is right for you. Use holiday leave or see if there is any weekend work available. Regard it as an investment in your future.

After undertaking some work experience, if you still believe this is the career for you the next step has to be looking at entry options and obtaining any qualifications that are necessary.

Ask yourself the following.

- ▶ Do you have the right qualifications to begin a career in business, finance and administration?
- ▶ Do you need any further training?

DID YOU KNOW?
Delivery times in Hong Kong can be delayed for an unexpected reason. Instead of traffic delays, there are elevator delays. It often takes people longer to travel vertically than horizontally as access to elevators is so congested during peak times. This is due to the sheer number of people living in high rise buildings.

- ▶ Can you get on the job training or do you need to attend a college course?
- ▶ How can you convince potential employers of your interest?

Use the further information section which follows to find answers to these and any other questions you may have. There are lots of organisations waiting to help you develop your qualifications and career prospects within an expanding industry.

THE LAST WORD QUIZ

So do you have the skills required to make a career in business, administration and finance?

Have a look through this final checklist to see if you are the right person for the job.

Tick yes or No

Are you a good time keeper?	☐ Yes	☐ No
Are you a very organised person?	☐ Yes	☐ No
Are you calm, patient, reliable, responsible?	☐ Yes	☐ No
Do you want an office based career?	☐ Yes	☐ No
Do you like working with figures and documents?	☐ Yes	☐ No
Can you communicate effectively and deal with all kinds of different people?	☐ Yes	☐ No
Can you use your initiative when required?	☐ Yes	☐ No
Do you have a knowledge of how businesses operate?	☐ Yes	☐ No
Can you back up your answers with evidence?	☐ Yes	☐ No
Are you happy working inside?	☐ Yes	☐ No
Are you prepared to wear business attire?	☐ Yes	☐ No

If you answered 'YES' to all these questions then congratulations! You've chosen the right career. If you've answered 'NO' to any of these questions then a career as an administrator may not be for you; however, there are still plenty of other jobs within business, finance and administration that may suit you better such as a financial controller or production manager, or think of setting up your own business.

CHAPTER 12
FURTHER INFORMATION

City & Guilds
www.cityandguilds.com

AQA / City & Guilds Diploma
www.diplomainfo.org.uk/AQA-City-and-guilds-diplomas.asp

Edexcel
Tel 0870 240 9800
www.edexcel.com

Edexcel is the UK's largest awarding body for academic and
vocational qualifications. There is a Subject Advisors Service which
can offer advice on qualifications in business, administration and
finance. They can be contacted on 0844 576 0036 or via email at
businessandadministrationSubjectAdvisor@edexcelexperts.co.uk

Connexions
www.connexions.gov.uk
www.connextions-direct.com/jobs4U

These sites provide careers information for young people and have
links to local Connexions offices. You can also find detailed job
descriptions and profiles of people working in different areas of
business, administration and finance, enabling you to gain a feel
for what a job is like.

Apprenticeships

For information about Apprenticeships contact your local Connexions Partnership or log on to www.apprenticeships.org.uk

England: www.apprenticeships.org.uk and your local Connexions office

Scotland: www.skillsdevelopmentsscotland.co.uk, www.modernapprenticeships.com. and Skills Development Scotland

Wales: www.careerswales.com and the DECYP and Careers Wales

Northern Ireland: www.delni.gov.uk/index/successthroughskills/apprenticeshipshipsni.htm www.careersserviceni.com and DELNI, Careers Northern Ireland

Careers Advice

www.careersadvice.direct.gov.uk/helpwithyourcareer/jobprofiles
A very useful website containing lots of information about careers, job profiles and advice on applying for jobs.

Learning & Skills Council
www.isc.gov.uk

This organisation is responsible for funding and planning education and training for over 16s in England. The website contains details of various training opportunities.

In Scotland this task is undertaken by the
Scottish Funding Councils for Further and Higher Education
www.sfefc.ac.uk

In Wales by the
Education and Learning Wales
www.elwa.ac.org.uk

Become instantly more attractive

To employers and further education providers
Whether you want to be an architect (Construction and the Built Environment Diploma); a graphic designer (Creative and Media Diploma); an automotive engineer (Engineering Diploma); or a games programmer (IT Diploma), we've got a Diploma to suit you. By taking our Diplomas you'll develop essential skills and gain insight into a number of industries. Visit our website to see the 17 different Diplomas that will be available to you.
www.diplomainfo.org.uk

In Northern Ireland by
The Department of Education
www.deni.gov.uk

UCAS
For information on degree courses in the UK
www.ucas.ac.uk

Training and Job Opportunities

Council for Administration
6 Graphite Square,
Vauxhall Walk,
London SE11 5EE
www.cfa.uk.com
Tel 020 7091 9620
This organisation is the leading UK authority on business and
administration. It offers advice on qualifications, careers in
business and administration plus details of how to apply for
apprenticeships and young apprenticeships.

Institute of Professional Administrators
6 Graphite Square,
Vauxhall Walk,
London SE11 5EE
www.inprad.org
Tel 020 7091 2606
This organisation is the major institute for administration and
office professionals. It provides training programmes and
qualifications.

IFS School of Finance
IFS House,
4–9 Burgate Lane,
Canterbury,
Kent CT1 2XJ
Tel 01227 818641
www.ifslearning.ac.uk

Financial Services, Accountancy and Finance
51 Gresham Street, London EC2V 7HQ
Tel 0845 2573772
www.fssc.org.uk
This organisation offers advice on careers and training
opportunities in the financial services.

Pathways
www.pathways.cii.co
This is a useful site offering information on career options within
financial planning, insurance broking, underwriting and risk
management, claims, mortgages, life and pensions work.

www.charterbanker.com
This offers information on banking qualifications.

www.breakinto.biz
This site contains lots of case studies about people working in
business, finance and administration showing what they do, and
how they have progressed their careers.

The Prince's Trust
www.princes-trust.org.uk
Offers help, advice and funding to young people starting up in
business.

Shell LiveWire
www.shell-livewire.org
The UK's biggest online community for young entrepreneurs. It
provides a forum for advice and discussion, a business library and
an opportunity to seek funds for new business ideas.

Business Link
Tel 0845 6090 9006
www.businesslink.gov.uk
Comprehensive business advice and support available online and
through local advisors. It contains a directory of organisations that
give grants and support to businesses.

Bright Ideas Handbook,
Which?
www.which.co.uk
This handbook shows how to develop, protect and make a profit from innovations.

Wealth Intelligence Academy (WIA)
www.wealthintelligenceacademy.co.uk
offers training and advice plus opportunities for networking.

Government Skills
This organisation works with government employers to identify skills needs and create suitable training programmes. It contains details of job vacancies with Government Skills, Operational Delivery and Professions Support Teams.

Central Government, First Floor, Kingsgate House, 66–74 Victoria Street, London, SW1E 6SW
Tel 020 3300 8977
www.government-skills.gov.uk

www.lgcareers.com
A useful website giving information on careers in local government.

www.jobcentreplus.gov.uk
Tel 0845 6055 255
This is an essential website for anyone looking to develop a career in local or national government. All government departments and most local authorities automatically post details of vacancies on this website. You need to look under specific categories such as Administration Local Government to identify what is available.